Welcome to Elsa Lopez's home!

What's in this book

学习内容 Contents   2

读一读 Read   4

听听说说 Listen and say   12

写一写 Write   16

多元学习 Connections   18

温习 Checkpoint   20

分享 Sharing   22

This book belongs to

_____

爱莎的新家 Elsa's new home

学习内容 Contents

沟通 Communication

介绍自己的住所
Introduce one's home

生词 New words

★	住	to live
★	层	storey
★	着	(used to indicate the continuation of an action or a state)
★	旁边	side
★	中间	middle
★	所	(measure word used for buildings, schools, hospitals, etc.)
★	向	towards
★	门口	entrance
★	方便	convenient

背景介绍：
爱莎搬新家了。

参观	to visit
介绍	to introduce
号码	number
开	to open
关	to close
姓名	full name

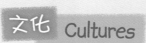 文化 Cultures

中国的传统建筑风格
Traditional Chinese building styles

句式 Sentence patterns

大门开着，窗户关着。

The door is open and the windows are closed.

参考答案：

1 Yes, they came and slept over./No, I have not.
2 It is a large house by the seaside./It has many rooms so that all of my family and friends can live in it.
3 They are moving into a new house.

跨学科学习 Project

设计一所未来式的住房
Design a house of the future

Get ready

1 Have you ever invited your friends to your home?

2 What does your dream house look like?

3 What is Elsa's family doing?

🎧 读一读 Read

故事大意：
朋友们通过找房子游戏找到了爱莎的新家并参观了爱莎的房间。

cān guān
参观

参考问题和答案：
The children get off near Elsa's new home. Can you guess what they are going to do? (They are going to visit Elsa's new home.)

大家去参观爱莎的新家。下车了，爱莎说："我们玩找房子的游戏吧！"

4

参考问题和答案：
1 How many storeys does the pink house have? (It has two storeys.)
2 What is the house number? (It is No. 3.)
3 Does Elsa live in this house? (No, Elsa lives in House No. 20. The woman by the window lives in this house.)
4 What is Elsa doing? (She is introducing her new home that her friends need to find.)

"开始介绍啦！我住的房子两层高，门牌号码是20号。"爱莎说。

"是中间这所房子吗？"艾文问。
"不是，要向前走。"爱莎说。

参考问题和答案：

参考问题和答案：

1 Is this Elsa's house? (Yes, because its house number is 20.)
2 Is the door open or closed? (It is closed.)
3 What is there next to Elsa's house? (There is a tree.)

"我家的房子是灰色的，大门关着，窗户开着，旁边有棵树。"爱莎说。

"这所房子是你家，因为门口写着你的姓名！"浩浩说。

参考问题和答案：
How does Hao Hao know this is Elsa's home?
(Because he sees Elsa's name on the door.)

fāng biàn
方便

参考问题和答案：

1 What does Ethan see through the window? (He sees their school.)

2 What does Ethan think about the location of the house? (He thinks it is convenient, because the house is near their school.)

3 Does Elsa like her new house? (Yes, she does. She looks very happy.)

"你的新家太漂亮了！离学校真近，真方便！"伊森说。

Let's think

1 **Recall the story. Tick Elsa's house.**

提醒学生观察第5至8页。爱莎的房子有两层高、灰色的、旁边有树，故选第二张图。

2 Which house do you like best? Discuss with your friend and tick your favourite one.

我最喜欢树上的房子，因为……

你喜欢高楼吗？

New words

1 Learn the new words.

一所房子

关着

门口　号码

开着　层

住

向这儿看。　旁边

介绍　中间　真方便！

姓名

参观

男子拿着语音导览器
在听画作的介绍。

2 Listen to your teacher and do the actions.

参考句子：
开窗。/关门。/向上看。/说出你的
姓名。/介绍你的爸爸。

写一个号码。

19

11

听听说说 Listen and say

提醒学生先用简笔画画出听到的录音内容，再根据图画作答。

1 厨房在第几层？

（a） 第一层   第一题录音稿：
b 第二层   1 这所房子有三层，第一层是客厅和厨房，第二层是卧室和洗手间，第三层是书房。
c 第三层

2 羊和狮子的中间是什么？

（a） 马   2 这是我画的画。狮子的前面是马，后面是熊。马的前面是羊。熊的后面是老虎。
b 熊
c 老虎

3 要去跳舞的同学怎么走？

a 向北走   3 大家好，要去跳舞的同学请向东走，要去做运动的同学请向西走。
b 向西走
（c） 向东走

04 **2** Look at the pictures. Listen to the story an

请问买文具要去第几层？

请到第五层，卖书的地方有文具。

中间这个文具盒真漂亮！

旁边那个绿色的也很好看。

第二题参考问题和答案：

1 Where can Ling Ling shop for stationery? (She can go to the bookshop on the fifth floor.)
2 Does Ling Ling like the bookshop? Why? (Yes, because she can buy stationery, toys and books. It is very convenient.)
3 Are the bookshops that you go to as convenient as this one? (Yes, I can also buy stationery, books and toys there./No, they are not.)

请问文具在什么地方？

向旁边看，文具在那儿。

你累吗？那儿可以坐着休息。

不累！这里可以买文具、玩具和书，真方便！

3 Write the letters and say.

a 坐着　b 中间　c 方便　d 旁边

1

我在外公和外婆的 ___b___ 。

2

我 ___d___ 的是谁？它是我的好朋友小白。

3

我们在门口 ___a___ 。

4

新年到了。上网买礼物很 ___c___ 。

13

Task

Play a game with your friends. Describe your home and ask the others to draw it. Then compare their pictures and see which one looks the most similar to your home. 参考表达见下方。

我住的楼30层高，是灰色的。我住在第10层。

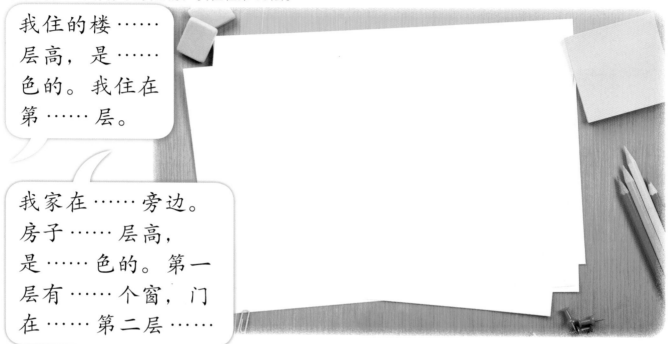

我住的楼······层高，是······色的。我住在第······层。

我家在······旁边。房子······层高，是······色的。第一层有······个窗，门在······第二层······

我家在学校旁边。房子两层高，是红色的。第一层有两个窗，门在中间。
第二层有三个窗。门口有一个花园，房子旁边还有一棵大树。

Game

Play with your friend. Choose a house, describe it and ask your friend to point it out. 可以让学生自己画房子，再玩猜房子游戏，以增加游戏的趣味性。

这所房子两层高，窗关着，门也关着，在黄色和蓝色的房子中间。

是这所红色的房子吗？

是的。

Chant

儿歌的第一段是问句，第二段是答句，先带学生朗读几遍儿歌，再让他们将第一段和第二段的问句和答句分别配对。

🎧 **05** Listen and say.

你的家门向着哪？
你家旁边有什么？
前面后面住着谁？
生活方便不方便？

我家门口向着南，
旁边是个小公园，
前面住着王先生，
后面有个火车站。
生活方便人友善，
东南西北都好看。

生活用语 Daily expressions

真方便。
It's convenient.

我来介绍一下，
这是……
May I introduce
you to …

写一写 Write

1 Trace and write the characters.

丿 亻 亻 亻 仁 住 住

住	住	住	住

提醒学生"住"字里"主"中间的一横是最短的，下面的一横是最长的。

丶 丬 门
丶 冂 口

门	口	门	口
门	口		

2 Write and say.

它 住 的小房子是黄色的。

这所房子 门口 的雪人戴了帽子和围巾。

16

3 Fill in the blanks with the correct words. Colour the roofs using the same colours.

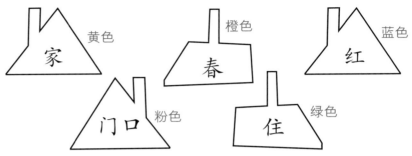

家 黄色
春 橙色
红 蓝色
门口 粉色
住 绿色

这是我的 家 ，我在这里 住 了三年。

我的 家 两层高，门是 红 色的。 门口 有很多花，到了 春 天非常好看。

拼音输入法 Pinyin input

提醒学生打字时在每个新段落前面都要缩进两个汉字的位置。

Write the letters in the correct place to complete the conversation. Then type it and role-play with your friends.

a 太好了，出发！   b 想去游泳吗？   c 去爷爷奶奶家吗？

"今天是星期六，我们去哪儿玩？ b "爸爸问。

"现在已经是秋天了，有一点儿冷，我不是很想去。"我说。

" c 他们的新家很近，可以走去。"妈妈说。

" a "我说。

17

多元学习 Connections

吊脚楼一般分两层，上层干燥通风，用来居住，下层用来饲养牲畜或堆放杂物。土楼是世界上独一无二的山区大型民居形式，有圆形、方形、长方形、五边形等形状。窑洞有厚厚的屋顶和墙壁，所以夏天隔热，冬天保温。蒙古包的设计方便拆卸移动，适合游牧生活。丹巴梭坡碉楼在四川省，建于民居旁的碉楼，平时用作贮藏室，也可在战时用于作战。

There are many different traditional building styles in China. Look at the photos, match them to the descriptions and write the letters.

这些楼真高！ e

这些房子会"走路"。 d

这个楼里住着很多人。 b

这里冬天暖和，夏天凉快。 c

这些房子两层高。 a

	Building style	Chinese name	Feature
a	Stilt houses	Diàojiǎolóu	usually built above the water on slopes
b	Earthern buildings	Tǔlóu	could have more than 100 rooms in each building
c	Cave dwellings	Yáodòng	arc-shaped, usually dug out of hillsides
d	Mongolian yurts	Ménggǔbāo	round tents, built to be transportable
e	Watchtowers	Diāolóu	very tall, usually built besides lower houses

通过问问题，提供多种角度供学生发挥想象。如：从构造方面（房子是用什么材料做的？是什么形状的？有多少层？）、从位置方面（房子是建在地球上吗？是在空中还是水底？）、从功能方面（房子会移动吗？会变大变小吗？会隐形吗？）。

1 What do you think houses in the future will be like? Design a house of the future. 引导学生理解智能房屋的功能。

这所房子可以用电脑关门。

这些房子可以用"太阳"做饭。

引导学生观察房屋顶的太阳能板。

你的房子呢？

这所房子会飞。

2 Role-play as a salesperson and sell your house idea to your friends. Whose house is the most popular one?

我来介绍一下，这所房子两层高，可以住三个人。住在这里很方便。冬天，外面下着雪，但是房子里面很暖和。夏天……

我想买这所房子，因为……

我觉得……

Eco-house

温习 Checkpoint

先参照游戏说明和所给的例子向学生解释游戏规则，再开始游戏。提醒他们在给方向指示时要配合方向标的方向。

1 Read the instructions and play with your friend.

北
西 ✦ 东
南

a Player A 😊 selects a number for Player B 😊. 😊 answers the question.

b 😊 selects a house in mind and guides 😊 to it in Chinese. 😊 traces the correct route.

c 😊 describes the house in Chinese.

d Switch roles and start a new round.

号码一，请写字。😊

❶

住 (to live)

向东走。

向南走。

这所房子是红色的，两层高，号码是10号。

❷

这是 门 口 。

向东走。

再向东走。到了。

这所房子…… 😊

这所房子的旁边有树。

❸

他们昨天做了什么？

他们昨天…… 去了动物园。

这所房子是绿色的，两层高。

❹

长颈鹿的旁边是什么？

长颈鹿的旁边是斑马。

这所房子的门开着，窗也开着。

Ann Jones

评核方法：

学生两人一组，互相考察评价表内单词和句子的听说读写。交际沟通部分由老师朗读要求，学生再互相对话。如果达到了某项技能要求，则用色笔将星星或小辣椒涂色。

2 Work with your friend. Colour the stars and the chillies.

Words	说	读	写
住	☆	☆	☆
层	☆	☆	🌶
着	☆	☆	🌶
旁边	☆	☆	🌶
中间	☆	☆	🌶
所	☆	☆	🌶
向	☆	☆	🌶
门口	☆	☆	☆
方便	☆	☆	🌶
参观	☆	🌶	🌶

Words and sentences	说	读	写
介绍	☆	🌶	🌶
号码	☆	🌶	🌶
开	☆	🌶	🌶
关	☆	🌶	🌶
姓名	☆	🌶	🌶
大门开着，窗户关着。	☆	🌶	🌶

Introduce one's home	☆

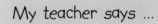

My teacher says ...

3 What does your teacher say?

评核建议：

根据学生课堂表现，分别给予"太棒了！(Excellent!)"、"不错！(Good!)"或"继续努力！(Work harder!)"的评价，再让学生圈出上方对应的表情，以记录自己的学习情况。

分享 Sharing

延伸活动：

1 学生用手遮盖英文，读中文单词，并思考单词意思；

2 学生用手遮盖中文单词，看着英文说出对应的中文单词；

3 学生四人一组，尽量运用中文单词分角色复述故事。

Words I remember

住	zhù	to live
层	céng	storey
着	zhe	(used to indicate the continuation of an action or a state)
旁边	páng biān	side
中间	zhōng jiān	middle
所	suǒ	(measure word for buildings, schools, hospitals, etc.)
向	xiàng	towards
门口	mén kǒu	entrance
方便	fāng biàn	convenient
参观	cān guān	to visit

介绍	jiè shào	to introduce
号码	hào mǎ	number
开	kāi	to open
关	guān	to close
姓名	xìng míng	full name

Other words

大家	dà jiā	everybody
下（车）	xià (chē)	to get off (a vehicle)
门牌	mén pái	house number sign
大门	dà mén	door
窗户	chuāng hu	window
棵	kē	(measure word for plants)
看见	kàn jiàn	to see
离	lí	to be away from

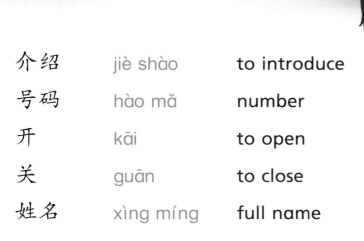

OXFORD
UNIVERSITY PRESS

Oxford University Press is a department of the University of Oxford.
It furthers the University's objective of excellence in research, scholarship,
and education by publishing worldwide. Oxford is a registered trade mark of
Oxford University Press in the UK and in certain other countries

Published in Hong Kong by
Oxford University Press (China) Limited
39th Floor, One Kowloon, 1 Wang Yuen Street, Kowloon Bay,
Hong Kong

Illustrated by Ah Lun, Anne Lee, Emily Chan, KY Chan and Wildman

Photographs for reproduction permitted by Dreamstime.com

China National Publications Import & Export (Group) Corporation is an authorized distributor of
Oxford Elementary Chinese.

Please contact content@cnpiec.com.cn or 86-10-65856782

ISBN: 978-0-19-082307-8

10 9 8 7 6 5 4 3 2

Teacher's Edition
ISBN: 978-0-19-082319-1

10 9 8 7 6 5 4 3 2